Contents

Welcome to Minecraft

It's an almost endless world of creativity, freedom and fun, where your imagination is the most powerful tool of all!

Minecraft is one of the most-played games of all time, and yet you'd do well to find two people who had the exact same experience in their own block-built world. With the ability to shape and create huge structures or mine the deepest caves for valuable resources, there's no right or wrong way to play Minecraft – it's totally up to you! Of course, without any missions or objectives to guide you, Minecraft does also pose the eternal question of 'What should I do next?'.

Over the following pages we'll guide you through the basics and offer up some fun ideas and tips on how to survive and thrive in a world that can be both deadly and delightful, depending on however you want to play it. Whether you're a miner or a crafter, we've got you covered!

CREATIVE MODE

This is the best way to play if you just want to build whatever you want to from the very beginning. Everything is unlocked as soon as you start a new game, so you'll have access to every block type, every cool feature and every tool you could possibly need. Plus, you're immortal (hostile mobs will leave you alone) and can even fly around the world – leaving you free to build the biggest and best Minecraft designs you can ever imagine!

FUN FACT
Even before it was officially released in 2011, Minecraft had more than 16 MILLION people playing it!

TIMELINE

2009 – First released to public (still in Beta stage)

2011 – Full version released + 1.0 Adventure Update

2012 – 1.1 to 1.4. + Pretty scary Update

2013 – 1.5 Redstone Update / 1.6 Horse Update / 1.7 The Update That Changed The World

2014 – 1.8 Bountiful Update

2016 – 1.9 Combat Update / 1.10 Frostburn Update / 1.11 Exploration Update

SURVIVAL MODE

This is Minecraft, the survival-exploration game. Here you can die (hostile mobs live up to the name!), you can't fly and you'll have to find and gather all of the resources you'll need to progress or build your next project. It's an epic adventure that will suit those looking for a bit more of a challenge (or a very tough one!), and it can be hugely rewarding. The good news is we've got a whole section dedicated to guiding you through it!

MULTIPLAYER

While you're free to go it alone, there's also a lot of fun to be had with friends in Minecraft. Whether it's teaming up for huge builds, or uniting forces to tackle the ender dragon, there are plenty of occasions where a little help can go a long way - with both split-screen and online options available for teaming up.

As well as providing a home for users to host their own servers, Minecraft also comes with its own 'realms' server system, but it does need a monthly subscription, so be sure you need it before spending any money.

MARKETPLACE

Speaking of money, the Minecraft marketplace is a huge shopping complex for fresh content, add-ons and even gameplay modes. This includes skins and texture packs to transform how your world looks, as well as mini-games and even entire adventures that drop you in a pre-built world with some tricky or creative challenges to overcome.

There's a huge amount to choose from, and it can all seem very tempting but it can quickly add up – so spend wisely and always make sure you've got permission from whoever is paying before clicking on anything!

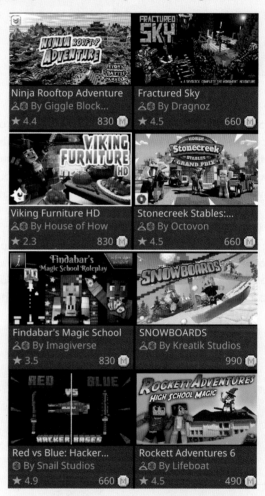

FUN FACT At the end of 2021, Minecraft-related videos passed a major milestone, with a combined total of more than 1 trillion views! That's 1,000,000,000,000!

2017 – 1.12 World of Color Update

2018 – 1.13 Aquatic Update

2019 – 1.14 Village & Pillage / 1.15 Buzzy Bees

2020 – 1.16 Nether Update

2021 – 1.17 Caves & Cliffs: Part 1 / 1.18 Caves & Cliffs: Part 2

2022 – 1.19 The Wild Update

STAY SAFE!

Survival mode can be quite intimidating for newcomers, so here are the key elements you'll need to get to grips with before heading into the great unknown.

HEALTH

Your health bar is indicated by the 10 hearts on your screen, which can be broken into halves to give you a total of 20 health points. Adding armour and the likes of enchantments or potions can give you added layers of protection to really boost your toughness.

If your health runs out and you die, you'll respawn at your last resting point, or your very first spawn point in the world if there isn't one, so you'll want to keep your health topped up at all times. To do so you'll need a steady supply of the following items.

TIP!

You're more likely to catch lots of fish when it's raining.

FOOD

You don't need to eat a lot, but food can still be very important. This is because having at least 9 out of your 10 food icons (those chunks of meat) filled will cause your health to regenerate, so any damage you take can be quickly healed with a nice snack. Your hunger bar only drops when you're active – so you won't burn off much walking around your base, but you will if you're mining or sprinting all over the place!

Early on, good foods include cooking up any raw meat from animals or fish in a furnace. Planting seeds to grow wheat can also make for an endless supply of bread. Some foods will give a bigger boost, or slow the rate your hunger drops, so give everything a try and see what suits your appetite!

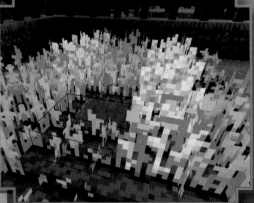

BEDS

As mentioned, when you die you'll either return to your original starting point in the whole game, or at your last 'respawn point' – and that's one very big reason to make a bed. Every time you interact with a bed it resets it as your new respawn point, so if you're travelling long distances a quick

snooze can save you being teleported hundreds of blocks back to the start if you stumble into trouble.

The other good reason for having one is that sleeping in a bed will fast-forward through the night (if you're playing with a day-night cycle) and can save you having to fend off any mobs that spawn.

LIGHT

It's easy to think that the monsters come out at night in Minecraft, but actually most of them simply come out when it's dark – which, yes, does include night-time, but it also means underground areas, or even dark rooms or a gloomy storm, can drop the light level low enough for mobs to spawn.

Thankfully you can quickly craft torches and find a host of other handy light sources to scatter around the world to brighten things up and stop those pesky monsters from coming out to play – so don't hold back and place as many as you can to keep yourself safe!

EXPERIENCE POINTS

In Survival mode, you'll collect little glowing orbs every time you kill mobs or mine certain resources. These are experience orbs that will fill up a green bar underneath your health, but you don't 'level up' with new perks as you may do with other games. Instead, your experience level is used more as a resource for enchantments, repairs and other upgrades, with a higher level generally unlocking more options during the various crafting processes.

You will lose all of your experience points if you die – although there is a five-minute window to recover everything from where you fell after you respawn – so don't be afraid to make the most of a good XP level while you can!

As for the whole combat, mining and crafting thing? We'll get to that in a little while.

TIP! You can only sleep at night, but you don't have to sleep in a bed for it to become a respawn point, as any interaction with it will be enough.

Y Inventory

TIP!
Cobblestone is very useful in the Nether, so it can be a good idea to keep a chest full of it nearby for a trip to the underworld or some other quick build.

BLOCKS

In Minecraft blocks are everything. They're what you mine and of course what you'll use to build with, and so you'll get to know a lot of them pretty well!

By now it's not exactly headline news to point out that Minecraft is a world built up of thousands and thousands of blocks. However, getting a better understanding of the many different types you'll find in the game can help you to live longer in Survival mode and sculpt even more daring designs in Creative!

THE USUAL SUSPECTS

Unless you dive straight into Creative mode's almost endless well of block options, dirt and cobblestone will be common building blocks for the early part of the game. This does make them a little less fashionable than some of the cooler stuff you'll get to later, but don't underestimate them. Dirt is great for building quick paths or defences that can be easily mined again, while cobblestone is an excellent fireproof building tool and it means you'll rarely be short of a stone sword or pickaxe.

ANTI-GRAVITY

Famously, Minecraft doesn't really deal with gravity quite as much as the real world, meaning blocks can be left suspended in mid-air. It can make it a bit of a nuisance to clean up an area at times, but you should also look at ways you can use it to your advantage. For example, lights hovering in the air can be used to illuminate open areas without getting in your way, or you can even build a base in the sky safe from the mobs below!

PRO-GRAVITY

There are some blocks which do adhere to the rules of gravity, most commonly the likes of sand and gravel. They're a reason why you should never dig straight up as they can cause damage if they fall on you. The upside is you can make the most of this, such as placing gravel blocks to fall down into a hole so you can drop into it. You can also combine anti- and pro-gravity blocks to good effect, such as setting a trap by placing sand on top of a dirt block to fall when the bottom block is removed.

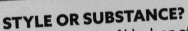

STYLE OR SUBSTANCE?

With many kinds of block on offer, choosing what to use for any given project can be tricky. In Survival mode, it's probably best to stick with what you've got a good supply of – so perhaps a log cabin if you're out in a forest, or a stone castle if not. In Creative mode you get more options, so can choose whether to go for the tougher materials, such as obsidian or End stone, or some more colourful options to really bring your builds to life.

A NEW LOOK

While everything is unlocked in Creative mode, survivalists will need to work a little harder to broaden their options. One thing to try is placing blocks in a furnace, as many can be given a makeover, while the crafting table can also lead to some interesting new choices. One early trick is turning sand into glass to give your home some windows or a giant sunlight (be warned, though, mining glass will cause it to shatter and drop nothing), but there are plenty more blocks to try, so play around and see what you can come up with!

TIP!
Wool can be a really fun building block as it can be easily dyed into many different colours, giving you a rainbow of options – but it isn't very strong.

TOOLS OF THE TRADE

Nothing should come between a good Minecrafter and their favourite pickaxe!

When it comes to combat and mining, having the right tool for the job is the difference between a quick finish and a slow grind. Not only does it matter to have the right object at hand, but also the material it's made with can affect its efficiency. Here's what you need to know to make sure you have the best gear at the right time.

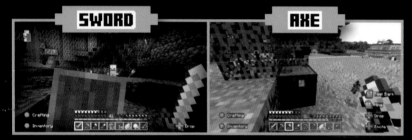

THE CORE FOUR

SWORD: Very much your melee weapon of choice, the sword also makes for a casual gathering tool, such as chopping down crops. This is because it's useless for just about anything else but fighting, so you won't accidentally dig a hole! Just be careful waving it around a passive mob, you could make it angry.

AXE: Use to quickly chop down trees and anything else wooden, the axe is also a handy back-up weapon as it does the second-most damage.

PICKAXE: Your core mining tool, the pickaxe is used to hack through most blocks with ease. Note that certain items, such as redstone and diamonds require at least an iron pickaxe to gather their resources, while obsidian can only be mined with a diamond pickaxe.

SHOVEL: Used to quickly clear through dirt and other soft blocks such as sand and gravel, the shovel is another constant companion for any mining or exploration project.

BETTER BY DESIGN

If you're playing in Creative mode, it doesn't matter too much what type of tool you use, as most blocks only take a single hit to mine regardless. However, in Survival the difference can be a matter of life and death. If you look at the list on offer when crafting, you'll see the order of wood, stone, iron, gold, diamond and netherite.

Each step offers a 1-point increase in damage across all tools and weapons – with the exception of gold, which looks great and can mine very quickly, but it is also as weak as wood for damage and durability. With diamond being rare and netherite only found in the Nether, establishing a good supply of iron weapons and tools is a very good start.

BEST OF REST

BOW: An essential ranged weapon that can keep enemies at a safe distance.

CROSSBOW: Working much the same as a bow, it has a longer charge-up period but fires arrows faster and further.

FISHING ROD: A simple tool to catch fish – and more – when used by water.

FLINT & STEEL: Can start a fire. Handy for a quick light source, but fire can spread quickly so use it wisely!

HOE: Used in farming to till, or prepare dirt to make it ready to plant seeds.

SHEARS: Can be used to trim wool from a sheep. You also get more wool than you would from killing them!

TIP!
Many tools will have alternate uses. For example, a shovel can dig a path, an axe can peel bark and shears can be used to gather grass, reeds and more. Keep an eye out for the on-screen prompts to see if there's something other than 'mine' on offer!

As for what makes the best weapons (in terms of base damage), there's another 1-point upward sliding scale, starting with the shovel as the lowest, then hoe and pickaxe tied, the axe and, of course, the sword as the best of the bunch. The bow and/or crossbow can deal more damage than a sword (up to 11 points with a fully charged hit for a standard bow), but there are a few other variables that can affect its power – not least having a good amount of arrows!

TIP!
We'll explain more later, but enhancements can make a huge difference to the power of any item, so don't wait too long to try some out!

GET CRAFTING!

The clue is very much in the title, but in Minecraft there are a lot of new resources and upgrades just waiting to be built so it pays to be a master crafter!

Although there's no real need for Creative mode users to craft very much, there's still a good feeling about turning a few items into something entirely new. The downside is that you'll need to enter the ingredients manually, whereas Survival mode comes with a recipe book that will help you mix up your new goods in no time!

CRAFTING TABLE

There are a few core items you can make on the move, most notably torches, but for the real good stuff you'll need to make a crafting table. This opens up pretty much everything, most importantly all of your key weapons and tools, as long as you've got the resources to match. They're easy to make, so be sure to drop several of them around your main locations with a well-stocked chest or two, so you can quickly restock your armoury or upgrade your base with a new item.

It's fairly straightforward to use once you get used to what tabs the various items come under, with a search option if you still can't find what you're looking for. It can take a while for the recipe book to fill up, so if you can't find something it might be that you haven't yet found a key ingredient – so check online for what you need and then go hunting!

TIP!
A good trick is to look through all the locked-out items that appear in red. You can see in the inventory window what ingredients you're missing so you'll know what to be on the lookout for.

FURNACE

Almost as important as the crafting table is the furnace. Not only can it cook raw food into a very healthy meal, it can also smelt your gathered ore resources, such as gold and iron, into ingots – which can then be crafted into weapons and other items. If you've got a big mining operation on the go, having several furnaces blasting away can save you a lot of time, but they do need a fuel supply so make sure you've got a good source of wood or coal to keep them burning!

TABLE MANNERS

You'll quickly find several more tables and other support items ready to be built and, if you've got the resources, it can pay to be curious to help you figure everything out. For example, you can make a cartography table to make maps (more on those a bit later), while a loom can be used to add cool designs to banners.

For your weapons, tools and armour, you might want to place an anvil to help repair anything with a low durability, while a grindstone can also repair items as well as removing unwanted enchantments. You'll need to wait a while to use it, but a smithing table will be needed to upgrade from diamond to netherite for the ultimate loadout.

STAY CRAFTY!

With the basics in place, you can also start to experiment with other construction items, such as hoppers, dispensers and a whole lot more. For example, one fun addition to any home is a jukebox to play music discs you may find on your travels. Parrots like music so it will give you both something to dance to! In Minecraft most things become easy once you know how, so don't be afraid to try out something new!

TIP!
If you can trick a skeleton into shooting creepers with an arrow, you stand a good chance of getting a new music disc.

KNOW YOUR ENEMY

The world is full of various friends and foes, with all non-playable characters known as mobs. Let's take a look at some of the more familiar faces.

The world of Minecraft can be filled with fun and wonder. On another day it can be a brutal onslaught of incessant and relentless combat that can stop you in your tracks. If you don't mind a little action, then the latter can be just as enjoyable, but you'll want to pick your fights carefully until you're confident facing off against some of the tougher enemies. Each biome will have its own unique blend of mobs, but here's an introduction to some of the regulars.

SPIDER

ZOMBIE PIGLIN

TIP!
Hostile mobs don't spawn in the mushroom fields biome, so if you want a safe place to set up a camp look for the huge mushrooms or large quantities in fields or on islands!

DROWNED

ZOMBIES

ZOMBIE ON FIRE

ZOMBIE VILLAGER

ILLAGERS AND PILLAGERS

These are human-like mobs that are most certainly hostile. You'll find illagers in the likes of woodland mansions, while pillagers can be found patrolling the wilds or in outposts. As well as attacking you – and often in a pack, which can be a challenge to fight off in one go – they also love to run raids on nearby villages. You can stand your ground and help the villagers if you like, fending off several waves of pillagers, with the chance to earn the 'hero of the village' status reward if you succeed. These guys are tough, though, so make sure you're ready!

ILLAGER

PASSIVE MOBS

The good news is that not everyone in Minecraft is out to kill you. You'll find many friendly villagers that you can trade with, as will the wandering traders you might come across in the wild accompanied by a llama or two. Likewise, you can also make good use of some animal companions. Whether it's creating a farm or taming a wolf who can prove a faithful friend and even help you out in a fight! Be warned, though. They might be called passive mobs, but if you provoke them you might find they become rather more hostile!

HOSTILE MOBS

For the most part, these include the various 'undead' mobs, such as zombies, skeletons and creepers, along with spiders and some other locals who are never happy to see you. Most of them will head straight for you, with the exception of skeletons who'll use their bows from afar.

Creepers explode and can wipe out your health bar if you're too close at the time, so tread carefully. The upside is most of these guys will catch fire in direct sunlight, making for very good mornings!

The further into the game you get, the tougher enemies will become,

with new ones introduced in the Nether, not to mention the wither and ender dragon. You'll find that most become predictable quite quickly, so just play it safe until you've got used to their routines and then use their weaknesses, and the environment, against them.

CREEPER

SLIME

FUN FACT

One figure you may never see is the urban legend of Herobrine. This is a character that has never existed in the main game, but his mythical status has seen him added to custom games and mods – and the name is still an in-joke among the developers and Minecraft community.

SKELETON

Puzzle Quest

A smart Minecrafter is a productive Minecrafter! So put your brain to the test with these fun teasers.

Messed Up Mobs

It looks like these Minecraft characters are a little confused! Can you unscramble them all and discover who's hidden behind the coloured squares?

ACROSS

2. HASTG
3. WRITHE
7. LIPING
9. MANNERED
10. RECREPE
12. ENDWORD
13. TWICH

DOWN

1. ZABLE
3. WANDER
4. ILLGRAVE
5. MOTHPAN
6. PRISED
8. KEENLOST
11. MOBZIE

The secret enemy is…

The Word Mine

Alex is in need of resources! Can you help her find everything she needs – and discover the one block type on her mining list that's not hidden in the grid? The words can be straight, diagonal and even backwards!

```
D R W A Q L A C N K E I J M N
O I A O D K E E T N K F M E B
P M R N L M T I O P O R A N R
G S H T E H E T R A I Y K O X
T R C R E T S E V O T L N T X
S I A R I E D N Y F N X H S F
G L I N L Y R O K D L O G D H
D T A B L X I T D I A M O N D
E R B M B I P S S J O F W A M
G O A I K C S W S Y C P I S D
C U S S K R T O D O H M P J D
G R A V E L O L T D X T Z I Z
S Z R B C E N G F L R Q E N T
U E V D S D E R L Q M R O M B
E N O T S D E R Z F V G M E A
```

AMETHYST	DIRT	GLOWSTONE	NETHERITE
COAL	DRIPSTONE	GRANITE	OBSIDIAN
COBBLESTONE	EMERALD	GRAVEL	REDSTONE
DIAMOND	GOLD	IRON	SANDSTONE

The missing block is...

A BIGGER WORLD

Quite literally the biggest change from the Caves & Cliffs updates (1.17 and 1.18) was the increase in height from 256 to 384 blocks. The clue is very much in the name, with 64 of those adding new depths to the game, and the other 64 opening Minecraft up to even higher mountains. Both areas were also given a visual makeover and several new biomes, such as lush caves, and several new mountainous sub-biomes such as meadows, frozen peaks and snowy slopes.

World update

This update makes your world higher and deeper. It adds more blocks and caves under your current world, so there's more to explore underground.

Make a backup copy of my world

Update and play

CAVES & CLIFFS

This two-part update introduced lots of new elements to the game, so here's a handy guide to what you might have missed!

MORE ORE

Copper is the game's first new ore since emerald was introduced back in 2012, and you'll find it in plentiful supply as you explore underground. It's primarily a building resource, as you can't use it to make new tools as you can with iron or gold, with copper blocks ageing over time to give a unique look to your builds. The update also introduced snake-like 'veins' to give more concentrated amounts of ore resources, making it a little easier to farm large amounts.

TIP!
You can coat copper with beeswax to give it a shiny green finish.

NEW BLOCKS

Lots of other new blocks were added as part of the update. If you've been playing recently the darker cobbled deepslate and dripstone will be familiar, with those pointed dripstone shards blocking a lot of underground routes. Caves now have vines and moss coverings, plus the likes of glow berries (which foxes love to eat!). In the mountains powder snow was added, which you can fall through, so tread carefully if you're heading out for a climb.

TIP!

Wearing at least one leather item will stop you from freezing in the new colder biomes, while leather boots will stop you falling through powder snow.

NEW MOBS

Another first for Minecraft saw the introduction of the axolotl, the game's first amphibian. It's based on the endangered Mexican salamander and can be found in the update's new lush caves. The update also added glow squids to underground water locations that drop glowing ink sacs, while the mountains are now home to goats – which can jump up to 10 blocks high!

BEST OF THE REST

There's plenty more in the update you might have missed, such as the lightning rod made using the new copper ingots. It emits a redstone signal when struck, so you can maybe use it to trigger something if you're getting creative with your builds! You'll also find cake-friendly candles as a fun, if low level, light source, while the new amethyst blocks play a note when you walk on them. Amethyst shards can be used to make tinted glass for some interesting designs and a spyglass to bring distant objects into view.

MANGROVE SWAMPS

Most of the new content is tailored to suit the two new biomes. The mangrove swamp is just that, a swamp filled with mangrove trees that add a new wood type, leaves and other items. Mud is also introduced in a solid form (it was previous only a liquid) and found in the biome. It can also be crafted using dirt and water, and then turned into mud bricks for a new building option, or dried out on dripstone to form clay.

GOING WILD

The Wild is the latest Minecraft update, adding two new biomes and fresh mobs – most are cute, but one can be very scary!

THE DEEP DARK BIOME

The clue is very much in the name with this new biome. Buried deep underground, it's likely to be one of the rarer locations, with mountainous areas a more common home to them. They can include an ancient city, that may contain some great loot, including the new Swift Sneak enhancement. You'll recognise the deep dark biome by the new green sculk blocks surrounded by moss-like covered blocks growing out of sculk catalysts that 'feed' on fallen mobs. There are also sculk shriekers that will react to your movement with a sonic scream. Trouble them too much and they might spawn the warden.

THE WARDEN

This is one very tough mob, capable of dishing out huge damage (with a large health bar of his own) with both a melee and a ranged attack, so if you're not equipped for a serious fight you'll want to steer well clear. It can also inflict a new Darkness effect, which temporarily darkens your vision, making it harder to see. The good news is that it's blind, but, while it can't see you, it can sense vibrations and smells, and will target any nearby player or mob that draws its attention. You can throw items as a distraction, and after a minute or so of relevant quiet, it will dig itself back underground again and you'll be safe... for a while.

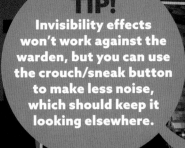

TIP!
Invisibility effects won't work against the warden, but you can use the crouch/sneak button to make less noise, which should keep it looking elsewhere.

FROGS SPAWNING

Among the new faces in the Wild update, are frogs and tadpoles. The latter can be carried around in a bucket and placed in water to hatch and grow into adult frogs over time. Frogs come in three colours, based on what biome they spawn in, and if you feed them magma cubes, they'll produce the all-new luminous froglights – with the colour of the light matching the colour of the frog.

INTO THE WILD

You'll also find the new allay, a friendly companion that you can give a block or item to and it will hunt for more. You'll most likely need to rescue them from a prison or pillager cage first, though. They're also joined by tiny fireflies that glow in the dark. At just two pixels in size, they're Minecraft's smallest creature yet!

Among the other new additions, you can now craft a recovery compass that will point to where you last died (as long as it's the same dimension), and you can also build a boat with a chest. It can only carry one person, but that's a lot of extra storage space to ship your supplies around between locations!

TIP!
Allays like music, so hitting a note block placed in your base will give them a 'home' to return to with their gathered goods!

TIPS FOR BRILLIANT BUILDING

Creative mode gives you the freedom to build and explore some amazing worlds, but what should you do when you can do anything? Here are some pro tips to consider.

PLAN AHEAD

You don't have to dive straight in when you get an idea to build something. Maybe sketch a rough design to help you see how it can look, or you could try mapping it out on graph paper first to help you count out how many blocks you want to use and make sure you line everything up just right.

CHOOSE YOUR LOCATION

Pyramids would look great in a desert but a wooden farmland might look a bit weird! However, you don't have to find the perfect spot for a build. With a little time and effort you can clean up any area to look just how you want it and give yourself plenty of room to work in.

THE FINER DETAILS

The first part of any project is to build the essential areas, but the second part is to add all the extra details, such as building a chimney above the fireplace, and putting in the smaller touches to make it look and feel more realistic. If you're building a house, look around your own home for ideas!

USE LIGHTS

You'll quickly get used to using lights to brighten up your buildings, both for being able to see in the dark as well as identifying it from further away if you get lost. However, you can also use lights to make your build stand out on a purely visual level and look cool from any distance.

TRY CIRCLES

TIP!
You can even try making your very own 3D model in advance by building a rough version with Lego!

Curves don't come naturally to Minecraft, so play around with techniques to make circular builds as well as the easier squares and rectangles, as it can really open up your build options. For example, think about recreating the Colosseum in Rome!

BUILD IT YOURSELF

Creative mode might unlock everything the game has to offer, but that doesn't mean you'll always find exactly what you need for your build. If you can't find the right block, there's nothing to stop you from making your own creations using the game's inventory, such as furniture or even things like trees!

HEAD FOR HEIGHTS

Building tall structures is easier in Creative when you can fly, but it can be easy to lose perspective, so keep the width looking natural, adding floors or intermitted levels for a realistic-looking building (think of the Eiffel Tower!).

BREAK THE RULES

Of course, Minecraft is a game where you can do whatever you like, so feel free to ignore all of this. Paint it all purple, build a house upside down, just do whatever makes you happy!

STARTING OVER

Don't worry if your build isn't perfect – it's all part of the learning process! Don't be afraid to start over as you'll pick up something new every time and make the next build that little bit better. In the same way, if you don't know how something works, just try it out! You might have to smash it up again, but it's a good way to pick up new tricks and ideas that will help you out with your next project.

FINDING INSPIRATION

You don't have to look too far to get some good ideas for your next potential build. Whether you want to recreate the pyramids, a football stadium or even try something fun like a ship on land or some large-scale pixel art, there's no limit to what you can do. If you do get stuck, use books, the internet or just look outside for ideas. You could recreate your own home, or even your whole neighbourhood – complete with a local supermarket stocked full of home-made crops!

SHIP AHOY!

This quick creation shows how it can help to lay down a basic frame before you start building upwards, and then you can add in some of the finer details to finish up!

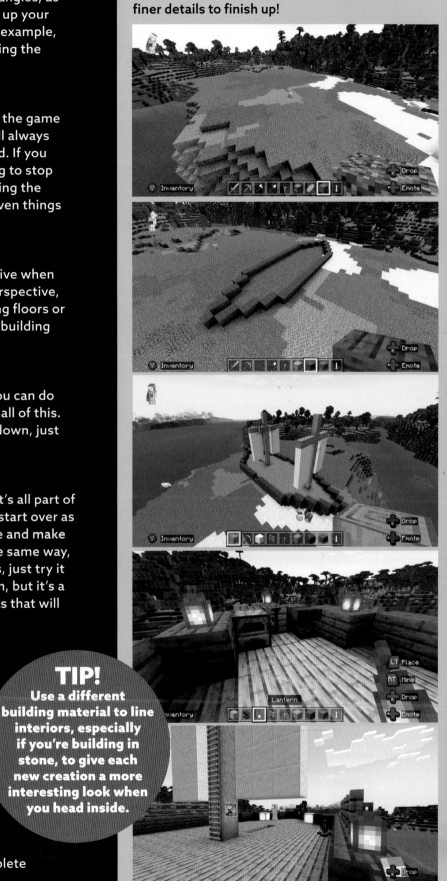

TIP!
Use a different building material to line interiors, especially if you're building in stone, to give each new creation a more interesting look when you head inside.

CIRCUIT TRAINING

Redstone plays a part in some of the most complex Minecraft moments, but it can also offer some simple solutions. Here's how it works...

CIRCUIT TRAINING

Redstone dust can be placed on top of most blocks, automatically connecting to any adjoining redstone or other powered items. You can't place it on a vertical surface, but you can link it upwards one block at a time like a carpet on a flight of stairs. Redstone can carry a signal up to 15 blocks, though other factors can impede on its power – a fully charged circuit will glow bright red, while an unpowered one will remain dark.

COLLECTING REDSTONE

Although you can buy it from traders or find it in some chests, you'll most typically find the best supplies when mining. Unsurprisingly, redstone can be found in the red-coloured blocks, but you'll need at least an iron pickaxe to harvest the redstone dust from it. You may find a good amount long before you really need it, so be sure to keep a good stash around ready for when you do.

TIP!
Redstone dust can also be used in brewing potions to make their effects last for longer.

IT'S ELECTRIC!

Redstone is effectively the heartbeat of Minecraft's power supply. Much like electrical wiring, it can carry a signal from a source to a destination, enabling you to trigger a switch in one place and see something happen elsewhere. It can be as simple as turning on a light or opening a door, or it can be hugely complicated – to the point where it's possible to build a working computer within the game!

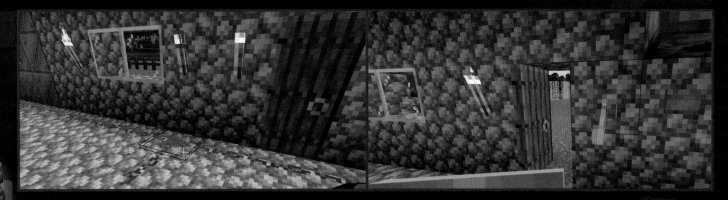

POWER SOURCES

To light up the redstone, you can place a permanent power source, such as redstone torches or redstone lamps, next to it, which will keep a constant signal. Alternatively, you can use the likes of a lever, button or pressure plate (all of which can be used without redstone, to open a door for example).

These will send a single pulse – the lever is a on/off switch, the button is a one-off trigger, and the pressure plate works when something, or someone, is placed on it. Other craftable items, such as observers, can also be used to trigger a signal – so play around and see what works!

SIMPLE SOLUTIONS

A quick example can be tried out by crafting a dispenser and placing it outside your front door – the idea being that you can fire arrows at any mobs that dare to come knocking. With the dispenser in place, you can fill it with arrows and then run a trail of redstone dust to a safe distance. Place a button at the end of the circuit and then every time you press it an arrow will be fired out. A pressure plate on the doorstep would automate the process, but you'll risk getting hit every time you use the door!

BUILD A BIN!

Things can get increasingly more complicated than this, with the likes of a repeater to extend the length you can run signals, for more complex circuits. One fun example is this rubbish bin, created by 'Adults Only Minecraft', that automatically deposits everything you place in the chests into the lava pit below (you can carry lava in a bucket, just like water). It requires a down-facing dropper with a hopper fixed on top and the chest above.

The circuit starts with a comparator next to the dropper, which recognises when something falls in. It then sends the signal to the repeater and back around to trigger a fresh drop that will repeat until it's empty.

This is a small example of what can be done, and should save a lot of hassle in getting rid of unwanted items. Once you've got the basics of redstone in place, there's no limit to what you can build!

HOW TO TAME ANIMALS

TIP!
Parrots will dance to music, so try crafting a jukebox in your home to get them moving!

The animals in Minecraft add a lot of colour and personality to most gameplay experiences, as well as providing lots of important resources. Taming them is a pretty simple process once you know their favourite foods, offering you an easy way to make some friends and keep your home stocked with useful supplies.

Some animals are limited to certain biomes, with the likes of wolves and foxes more common to taiga regions, while goats like mountains, parrots and ocelots stick to jungles and you'll find more horses in a savannah. This does mean you might need to roam around to find every animal type (or just spawn them yourself if you're in Creative mode), or maybe you're just as happy with different pets or companions in each new playthrough based on your spawn point.

To tame most animals, you just need to feed them their favourite food. If successful, you'll see love hearts pulse out from them – which also puts them into love mode. If you do this to a pair of the same animal, they'll instantly produce a new baby. The new-born takes around 20 minutes – the same as a full day cycle – to grow into an adult.

Once tamed, wolves will follow you around unless you instruct them otherwise and will attack some enemies, making them a good ally (or distraction) while you're out exploring. Cats and ocelots are also oddly good at scaring away phantoms and creepers! You can get other animals to follow you by holding their favoured food in your hand – enabling you to lead them back to your home or manoeuvre them into a fenced enclosure if you're building a farm.

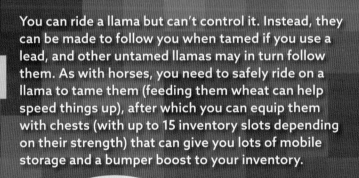

TIP!
You can dress llamas up with different coloured carpets for a cool and unique look!

You can ride a llama but can't control it. Instead, they can be made to follow you when tamed if you use a lead, and other untamed llamas may in turn follow them. As with horses, you need to safely ride on a llama to tame them (feeding them wheat can help speed things up), after which you can equip them with chests (with up to 15 inventory slots depending on their strength) that can give you lots of mobile storage and a bumper boost to your inventory.

You don't have to worry about feeding any of your new furry friends, so you're free to tame as many as like and just leave them to randomly roam around your game world. Or, as you will find out in a few pages time, you might want to build them a home of their own.

FAVOURITE FOODS

Use these to get animals to follow you or enter love mode!

Bees	Flowers
Cats	Raw cod / raw salmon
Chickens	Seeds
Cows	Wheat
Foxes	Sweet berries
Horses	Golden apples / golden carrots
Llamas	Hay bales
Ocelots	Raw cod / raw salmon
Pandas	Bamboo
Parrots	Seeds
Pigs	Carrots / potatoes / beetroot
Rabbits	Carrots / golden carrots / dandelions
Sheep	Wheat
Turtles	Seagrass
Wolves	Bones (tame) and raw meat (love mode)

Go Horse Riding!

HOW TO FIND YOUR PERFECT NEIGH-BOUR!

It can take a little time and effort, but having a really good horse can be a great way to get around your Minecraft worlds.

They're a lot easier to manage than a complex minecart system and offer a super-fast way to navigate the map, so if you're planning for an adventure, a horse can be a very trusty steed! They typically spawn in warm areas with large open spaces, so savannahs and plains are prime locations to search, while any grassy regions that aren't thick with trees may also see horses running free.

HORSE BACK

To tame a horse, you just need to mount it. The problem is that it may well try to throw you off, so you might need to climb back on a few times. You won't see the same hearts you get with other animals, but you will see its health bar appear on your HUD when it's tamed. However, while it's happy to have you on its back, you won't be able to control it without a saddle, and they can be tricky to get hold of.

SADDLE UP

Unfortunately, you can't craft a saddle, which means you might need to play the game for a while until you find one on your travels. There's a 1% chance of catching one while fishing, but you can also find them in chests hidden away in the likes of dungeons, strongholds and fortresses. You can also trade for one if you find a village with a leather trader of a good enough level. When you do get your hands on one, you can mount your horse and equip the saddle via the inventory.

TIP!
You can craft leather armour for added protection for your horse. Stronger armour can't be crafted, but it can be found in chests or traded with villagers.

TIP!
Saddles can be hard to find, so be sure to grab it each time you get off your horse in case it wanders off or gets killed while you're busy elsewhere!

MAKE A THOROUGHBRED

Horses are rated on three key attributes: speed (5-14 blocks per second), jump height (1 to 5.5 blocks) and health (15-30 hit points). These aren't all made readily available, so a little testing is required to get a rough idea of what each horse has. You can breed horses using golden apples, with the baby foal getting attributes that are an average of their parents and their own third, random number. By finding (or breeding) horses with high ratings, with a little luck, or a bit of trial and error, you can combine them into one super-horse to get the fastest, toughest ride in town!

PIGGY BACK RIDE

If you fancy something a bit different, one fun quirk of Minecraft is the ability to ride a pig! You just need to drop a saddle on them, while the trick to controlling them is to craft and equip a carrot on a stick (you can guess the ingredients!). Wherever the stick points, the pig will follow!

1 You can make it easier to find your way home by leaving a trail of some kind. Torches or other light sources are great for spotting at night, while simple pillars of dirt can also be seen from a good distance.

HOMEWARD BOUND

LIGHTING THE WAY HOME

A NEW DAY

TOP TRAVEL TIPS

One of the best parts of Minecraft is heading out and finding new places, but it's not without its risks. Here are some pointers to stay safe out there!

2 Keep an eye on the sky! As in the real world, the sun (and the moon) rises in the East and sets in the West, so you can use it as constant guide to give you a good sense of direction and time.

SUNDIAL

3

MAKING A BED

When you're planning a long trip, take a bed with you and use it often to reset your spawn point and avoid being teleported back to your base if you die. Plus, it helps you skip through the night to avoid lots of those pesky mobs!

4 Start small. Your primary objective when you start exploring is to be able to find your way back home again, so begin by getting to know your surrounding area and landmarks that will help you get your bearings.

5 If you're using the same few hub areas, you can establish clear links by building quick paths with a shovel, using cobblestone to make 'roads' to follow, and maybe even set up a minecart rail network. You can also add signs to help point any visiting friends down the right path!

6 One good early trick using the sun as a natural compass, is to head out in a single straight direction (such as due North) and then you know to do the opposite to return (head due South). Just be careful you don't get side-tracked!

7 Build regular mini-bases. They only need to be a quick build, housing maybe a bed, a crafting table and a furnace (and maybe a chest for storage), and will give you plenty of welcome stopping-off points on your travels.

A MINI-BASE

8 Pack some essentials but be wary of taking something you don't want to lose if you're in Survival mode. Food and lots of torches are a must, but do you really need to risk taking your only diamond sword?!

9 When you're on the move, be prepared to drop lesser items to make room for the good stuff. You can 'drag' items out of your inventory menu to throw them away.

10 Underwater explorers should look to loot a heart of the sea, as this can be used to craft a conduit to improve your powers and restore your oxygen level.

ON THE UP!

11 A quick way to get a bird's eye view or reach high-up items (like the top blocks of a mined tree) is to build a lift by jumping up and immediately placing a block directly under your feet. Repeat to go up and mine to go down!

12 A similar trick can be done using a bucket of water to create a waterfall from the top of a cliff that you can swim up and down – not forgetting to place a pool of water at the bottom so you don't damage yourself.

13 If you get lost while exploring underground, dig upwards. It's a lot easier to regather your bearings above ground and spot some familiar landmarks.

14 It's not something you'll be able to access early on in Survival mode, but ender chests and shulker boxes make it easier to transport large quantities of supplies all around your world.

15 If you're planning on taking a boat trip, a map, ideally a locator map, can be crucial to keep track of where you are without the aid of natural landmarks. Find out how to make one over the page...

BOAT TRIP

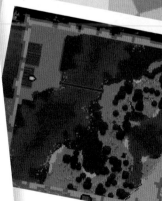

MAP

CRAFTING A MAP AND COMPASS

DON'T GET LOST!

With a world as huge as **Minecraft**, and one that's effectively randomised with each new game, it can be easy to get turned around and lose your bearings. Although you won't need them all the time, it can save you a lot of panicked searching to have a map and compass at hand to help you find your way if you do find yourself in unfamiliar surroundings – at least until Mojang gives us a sat-nav!

With a couple of easily-made items in your inventory, you'll always know where you are and where you're heading!

ON HORSEBACK

RAISED VIEW

1X ZOOM

FULL ZOOM

To make a map you just need some paper, which is crafted from sugar cane. You need 9x paper to make a map, which will be blank at first. There might not be a visual prompt but pressing the 'use' button while holding it will pop it up and it'll immediately fill in with everything in the nearby area.

TIP: The map will always appear with North at the top, which can help with your general navigation.

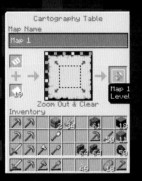

To enlarge the map, you can craft a cartography table. Using this, you can add more pieces of paper to the original map, increasing its range up to four sizes, with the final stage turning your original map into just a tiny corner of it, so don't go for the full-size too early! Any empty areas of the map will be filled in as you explore. In order for a map to be filled in, you need to have it in your possession as you travel, meaning any new changes to a location won't be shown on it unless you've taken that specific map back to the same spot.

Once you have access to iron and redstone, you'll be able to make a compass. Once crafted it's worth noting that, unlike real compasses that always point North,

in Minecraft they instead point towards your original spawn point – which is why it's usually a good idea to build a base close to that starting spot, so if you do get lost you've got a handy landmark for the compass to guide you towards!

With a spare compass, you also have the option to craft it into a locator map, which not only fills in as you explore, but also adds location markers to make key spots even easier to find later in the game. You'll appear on the map as a white outline that will move when you do, but you won't be centred on the map like in other games – meaning you can walk off the edge of its border into unknown territory.

VIEW OVER TREES

TIP: You don't need to equip the compass to use it. You can see it working if it's just placed in your quick-access hotbar for hands-free navigation.

COMPASS

You can also find or trade some explorer maps or treasure maps on your travels. These reveal the location of some nearby sites of interest (such as woodland mansions and monuments) or some valuable rewards worth seeking out. They should be reasonably close by, but if they are further away the player icon on the map will be smaller than usual as a hint that you've got a long trip ahead of you!

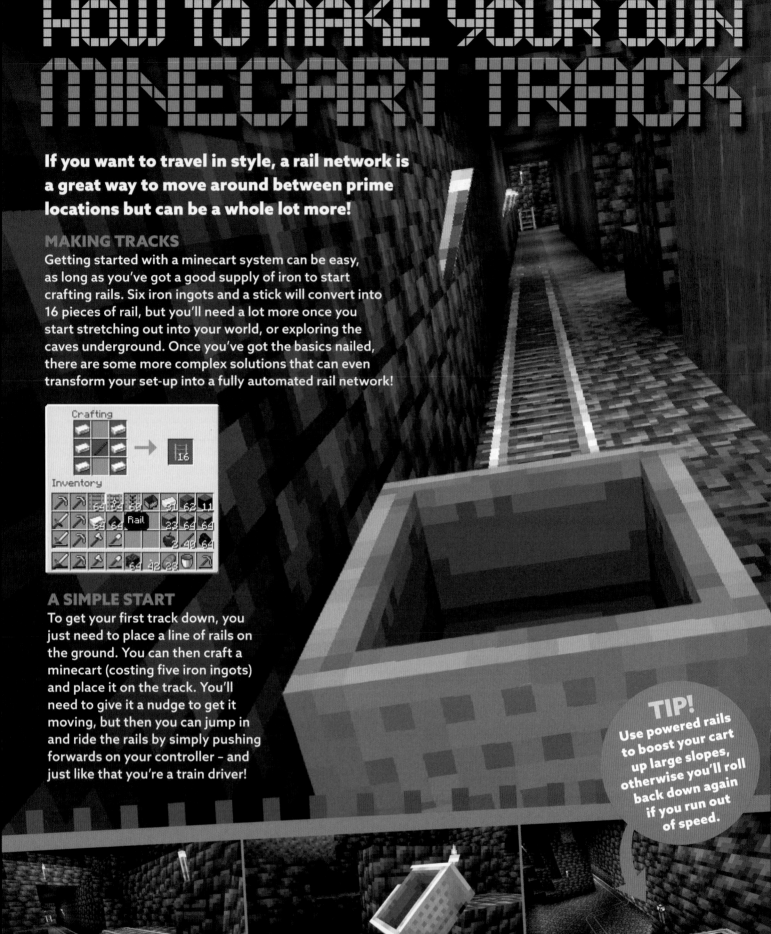

HOW TO MAKE YOUR OWN MINECART TRACK

If you want to travel in style, a rail network is a great way to move around between prime locations but can be a whole lot more!

MAKING TRACKS

Getting started with a minecart system can be easy, as long as you've got a good supply of iron to start crafting rails. Six iron ingots and a stick will convert into 16 pieces of rail, but you'll need a lot more once you start stretching out into your world, or exploring the caves underground. Once you've got the basics nailed, there are some more complex solutions that can even transform your set-up into a fully automated rail network!

A SIMPLE START

To get your first track down, you just need to place a line of rails on the ground. You can then craft a minecart (costing five iron ingots) and place it on the track. You'll need to give it a nudge to get it moving, but then you can jump in and ride the rails by simply pushing forwards on your controller – and just like that you're a train driver!

TIP!
Use powered rails to boost your cart up large slopes, otherwise you'll roll back down again if you run out of speed.

NAVIGATING TERRAIN

Of course, Minecraft isn't all even terrain and nice straight lines, so while it can be a good idea to mine tunnels or flat paths for your rail to speed through, you can adapt your track to the world around you. Rails will automatically slope up or downhill, one block at a time (with slopes slowing down or speeding up the cart), and to make turns you just lay the track at a right angle and the game will curve it to fit. If you want, you can make a zig-zag of curves to create a 'diagonal' track that the minecart will pass across as if it were a straight line.

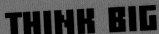

OTHER TRACKS

Powered rails are great as they give your cart a boost as long as they've got a nearby power source, such as a redstone torch. Without power, a powered rail will quickly slow the cart, making for a good stopping option. A boosted cart will naturally slow down over time, so having a three-block sequence of charged-up powered rails every 15-20 blocks will keep your minecart speeding around the world!

Detector rails trigger a redstone signal when your cart passes over it – offering up some useful creative options. Activated rails are similar but, besides ejecting anyone inside the cart when powered up, can be used to set off TNT minecarts or turn hoppers off – with unpowered activated rails turning them back on, for some interesting resource collection systems.

GET EXPERIMENTING!

These extra rails can be used to create complex but incredibly useful automated rail systems for moving resources around. One simple starting idea is to create a quick-start departure area for your track. This works by placing a down-sloped powered rail, with a redstone-powered button next to it. When you drop the cart onto it, the rail will hold it in place until you press the button to power it up – which will then give you a cool boost to set you on your travels! You can repeat a similar trick at intervals along the track and give you stopping-off points on the same line.

TIP!
You can use levers to make an interchange, flicking it to turn a T-shaped line one way and then the other.

THINK BIG

Creating a simple line between two key locations is a great first track to build, but there's plenty more you can do. Having multiple routes in your mines can make for an easy way to get around and transport resources (you can craft a minecart with a chest for extra inventory slots), and also help with navigation. So, if you've got the supplies, why not expand your rail network, or try one-off specials like a fun miniature railway or even a giant rollercoaster!

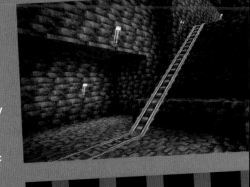

1

X Crafting

Y Inventory

A GOOD START
Be on the lookout for caves or ready-made holes that will save you a lot of time compared to starting a mine from scratch.

Hot Picks!

With many different methods, there isn't really a 'best' way to mine efficiently, but these tips should help you to figure out what works best for you!

2

CLOSE TO HOME: To save time and avoid outdoor mobs, starting a mine from inside your main base can be a good move. Although you might want to include a door or two to stop underground mobs from following you home!

3

LEAVE A TRAIL: It can be easy to get lost in a network of tunnels and caves, so come up with your own system to find a way back. You can craft signs, add stairs or use cleanly-mined trails through core paths. One trick is to always place torches on the left side of a tunnel (so they'll be on the right when you travel back).

4 TAKE STEPS: Digging diagonally down, one block at a time, will let you place stairs to help you get up and down quicker.

5 SAFETY LADDERS: You can use ladders to dig straight down, but there is a risk of falling. However, ladders are always useful to get you to safety if you do fall down a hole or need a quick route back to the surface.

6 DRY LAND: When starting a mine, be sure to dig away from any large water sources, to reduce the risk of accidentally flooding your hard work.

7 HOT PROPERTY: Diamonds can be hard to find in some of the deeper regions of the world. One good place to look is near large lava pools. Mining horizontal tunnels branching out from these areas, often reveals diamonds and other rare resources.

8 MINE SMART: You never know if there might be a big hole beneath your feet, so don't dig out the block you're standing on. Similarly, avoid mining directly above you in case lava, gravel or something else falls down.

9 LEVEL HEADED: When mining, be sure to leave a few stop-off points on the way down (maybe every 15 levels or so) to mine horizontal shafts from. You'll find different resources are more common at different depths, and it will give you new avenues to explore later on.

10 AIM HIGH: Although rare resources are typically found the deeper you go, you can also find the likes of emeralds (and lots of iron) buried within the higher mountains, so mining a path inside some peaks can also be very rewarding.

11 LISTEN UP: When you're mining a fresh path down, listen out for the tell-tale sounds of nearby enemies, as this indicates that there's a cave or some other opening close by that you might want to head towards.

12 QUICK BLOCKS: Keeping a basic block such as dirt or cobblestone in your quick-access inventory can be useful for a quick fix if you do accidentally dig into a water or lava pool. Plus, they can be used to keep mobs at bay or to make a quick bridge to nearby resources.

13 CARRY A TORCH: Actually, carry lots of them. Mobs will continuously spawn in the darkness, so be sure to fill a cave with lights before mining unless you're up for a fight!

14 BRING SUPPLIES: If you're planning a long underground trip, you should pack a good supply of food, plus maybe a crafting table to replenish broken tools, and a bed for a respawn point. In large caves you can even build a mini-base of operations to save repeated trips back to the surface.

15 THE ANTI-MINE: After exploring a large tunnel network, trying digging a path upwards to the surface to see where you come out!

REDSTONE

COPPER, COAL & IRON

GOLD

IRON

LIVING WITH ANIMALS

As well as all of the mining and crafting, you might fancy a quieter life with some of the friendlier, and furrier locals.

We've already looked at taming animals, but it can be well worth taking this to the next level by creating your very own wildlife reserve in your Minecraft world. Besides the irresistible cuteness of being surrounded by the likes of sheep, cows and chickens, it also provides a near limitless supply of their resources such as wool, leather, milk, and eggs – and, whisper it quietly, meat.

You don't have to build a barn or even fence the animals in place, although it can make things easier! Plus, it can be an interesting mini-project if you wanted to take a break from mining or exploring. As part of the building process, you might at least want to put a few barriers in place to keep possible predators at bay or perhaps to stop your furry friends from wandering off a cliff. They're happily self-sufficient but not always the smartest!

If you have access to a good supply of trees, a large wooden barn can be a great-looking addition to any Minecraft home. You can keep it simple or turn it into a fun playhouse for the animals to roam around – just don't forget to make sure it's well lit to stop mobs from spawning inside!

Wooden fences are quick and easy to make, so feel free to create an area that will keep the animals safe from harm and stop them straying too far away. Of course, you'll need a gate or two as well, so you can get in and out. You can create one large open enclosure or several smaller ones for each animal type. Many animals will follow you if you have their favourite food in your hand, so it's easy to lure them into place.

GROWING YOUR FLOCK

With just a few animals in place, you can start feeding to get them to make new baby animals, which will quickly grow into adults – you can speed up the growing process by feeding infants the same favourite food. Before long you can have a whole field-full of pets, providing you with some cute companions and lots of very useful resources at hand whenever you need them!

GROW YOUR OWN CROPS

Not many people will start playing Minecraft to be a farmer, but it's a fun and easy way to deliver a never-ending supply of food and lots of great crafting options!

HEY HOE!

To start farming you'll need to craft a hoe. This is used to 'till' dirt and make it ripe for planting seeds. You'll probably need to make a bucket as well, as you'll have to carry in a water supply to help your plants grow. Water can pass through up to four blocks, so filling a few well-placed holes should be enough to cover quite a large area (one water block in the centre can cover a 9x9 grid). You also need good light, so make sure your crops aren't over-shadowed by trees or buildings.

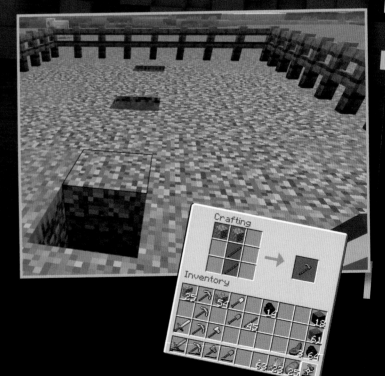

START SMALL

You don't need a lot else to start your first farm. You'll probably have picked up some plain green-coloured seeds from hitting grass in your general early gameplay, which will grow into wheat that you can craft into some tasty bread. Harvesting crops like wheat will provide both the final resource and more seeds to replant, while planting just one carrot or potato will harvest up to four, so you can replant those to quickly increase your yield and expand your farm.

GROW AND GROW

To plant seeds, you just need to have them in your hand and then press the use button (hold it down for a fast dispersal). Soil that's fertile should turn a slightly darker colour, but you might find the odd block needs to be re-tilled from time to time, so be ready to make a few quick fixes. You'll quickly learn to recognise when something's fully grown (wheat turns a slightly lighter yellowy-brown, for example), so just keep harvesting and re-planting! As your yield increases, you can either expand your existing farm or add additional plots for different crops as you grow.

TOP OF THE CROPS

The best crops might differ based on what you need, but wheat is always good as an easy food supply. Potatoes are a tasty treat, while carrots can be crafted into golden carrots which are useful in brewing potions. Sugar cane provides both sugar and paper, so it's also good to have a steady supply close by, and pumpkins can be used to make cool Jack-o-lanterns for some nice lighting features. You'll also find some biome-specific crops, plus the likes of Nether warts in the Nether, so feel free to work with whatever you've got at hand!

TIP!
You don't need to fence in your farm, but it can help prevent mobs from getting too close, and maybe stop a creeper from blowing up your crops!

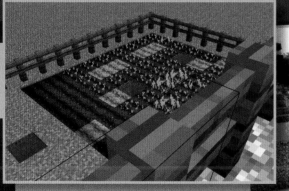

TIP!
Some crops will require different treatment. For example, sugar cane needs to be directly next to water, but it doesn't require tilled soil and can also grow nicely in sand. Whereas you might need to craft pumpkin seeds from fully-grown pumpkins to keep those supplies ticking over.

BUILD AN AUTO-HARVESTER

A fun way to save time harvesting your crops with a fully-automated sugar cane farm!

This quick build, based on a design by DoubleXP.com, works by using observers to see when the crop is grown, which triggers the pistons to punch out all but the bottom block of sugar cane - which will then regrow and repeat the process on an endless loop. A hopper minecart running underneath will suck up all the fallen sugar cane and drop it off into the chest below.

You will need Nether quartz to craft the observers, so you might need a trip to the Nether if you're playing in Survival mode, but once it's up and running you'll have an endless supply of sugar cane ready for whenever you need it!

1 To start with, you'll need to place a chest with a hopper feeding in to the back of it. Then, using your favoured block of choice, build a wall outwards from the hopper in each direction as far as you like – we went for five blocks each side.

2 On top of this wall, you'll need to place some rails. You'll want to place a powered rail at each end (with the likes of a redstone torch to power it), with normal rails filling in the rest of the line. Place a block at each end of the line to act as a stopping point, and then you can place a hopper minecart on the track. Give it a nudge and it will start on an endless back and forth along the line.

3 Next, you'll need to start building up a frame. The first aim is to get a row of sand or dirt blocks directly above the moving minecart, where you can plant your sugar cane. Of course, it will need a water supply, so build a trough behind the sand blocks and then fill it using a bucket, so that the water is in contact with the sand.

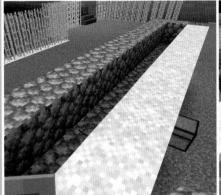

4 Building up a little higher, place a row of pistons directly behind but two blocks up from the row of sand – so that they'll be in line with the second block of grown sugar cane. On top of the pistons, place a row of observers, making sure everything is facing towards the front.

5 To create the required circuitry, you simply need to place a line of redstone dust on top of some blocks directly behind the pistons. The dust will be sparked into life when the observers above see the crop reach its eye-line and send the pistons firing forwards.

6 The final touch is to place some glass blocks in front of where the crops will be, just so that nothing gets punched outside the reach of the hopper minecart passing below. Everything collected will be funnelled down into the chest at the bottom, so all you need to do is to return from time to time to collect your harvested crops!

You can add your own finishing touches to the build, and perhaps look to extend it when you're able to craft more observers and pistons – although you will need to add extra powered rails in the middle to keep the cart moving when it gets up to around 20 blocks wide. There are several other methods you can adopt for farming all manner of crops, so there's no reason why you can't find bigger and better ways to take the strain out of farm life!

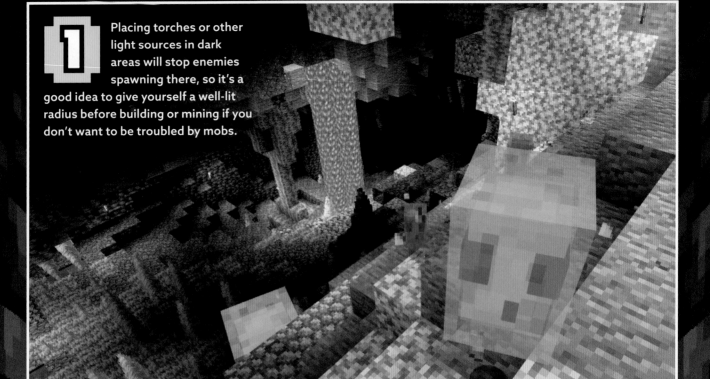

1 Placing torches or other light sources in dark areas will stop enemies spawning there, so it's a good idea to give yourself a well-lit radius before building or mining if you don't want to be troubled by mobs.

Fighting Talk

Outside of Creative mode or Peaceful difficulty, you're going to have to fend off some relentlessly hostile mobs. These tips should get you ready to rumble!

2 Most enemies aren't too smart, so use their flaws against them, such as leading them into lava traps or just placing blocks as obstacles to make it easier for you. Using narrow tunnels also lets you tackle multiple enemies one at a time.

3 A good sword is a must, and armour if you've got the resources. Iron is good, diamond is great, but netherrite is the best. And always carry at least one spare in case it breaks!

4 Your sword will have a greater range than most standard enemy melee attacks, so with good timing you'll be able to hit them before they can get close enough to hurt you.

5 As a further back-up, have your axe in the quick-access bar next to your sword to quickly swap to if it breaks. It's the next best weapon in your toolset, and in some versions of the game the axe is even more powerful.

6 A ranged bow or crossbow can also be useful to pick off enemies without risking toe-to-toe combat. If you can find a few blocks of high ground, zombies can be powerless to stop you.

7 A shield is always a good option to have. It can absorb and even deflect a lot of damage, sending skeleton arrows straight back at them!

8 Enchantments can also make a big difference, both to the damage you dish out (such as Sharpness) and what you take (Protection), so try them out to toughen yourself up even more.

9 You can place items such as a cactus or cobwebs around your bases to hurt or slow down any approaching enemies, making them much easier to pick off.

10 Watch your back! It's easy to focus on what's in front of you and miss a creeper sneaking up behind, so take a quick look around before and after each encounter.

11 Some enemies have hits that will knock you backwards, so try to avoid combat near large drops or somewhere a creeper explosion could wipe out the floor you're standing on.

12 Speaking of creepers, either use a bow or you'll need to back up after each hit to stop them from exploding. Although you can also exploit their destructive tendencies to help mine a good-size area!

13 Run away! You'll be faster than most enemies, so if your health is low, or perhaps dropping fast after getting hit by a witch's potion, quickly dash to a safe spot to recover and regroup. If death looks inevitable, try to at least rush to a spot where you have a better chance of recovering your supplies.

14 If you do get hit by a potion or something similar, a bucket of milk will remove any status effects, so it can be a strangely useful item to keep in your inventory.

15 In a tough battle, the likes of steak, cooked porkchops or golden apples/ carrots are among the best recovery foods, as they'll reduce your hunger bar slower and keep your health topped up for longer!

HOW TO MAKE YOUR BEST GEAR AWESOME!

Enchantments can seem like a rare luxury item, but it doesn't take too much work to be able to transform your inventory with some super-charged upgrades.

THE ENCHANTING TABLE

The most common way to create and apply enchantments is by making yourself an enchantment table, which requires some obsidian, a couple of diamonds and a book. Make sure to place it somewhere with a good few blocks of space around it, as you can add bookshelves over time to boost the potency of your enchantments, with many of them coming with several levels of increasing power.

COOK THE BOOKS

Making bookshelves requires paper and leather. You can get the former from sugar cane and the latter from cows – so setting up a farm for both early on can be very useful, as you can place up to 15 of them. The closer to the enchantment table they are, the better the effect, but you need to leave at least one block of space between them. This means the best set-up is having the table in the centre and the bookshelves around it in a 5-block square radius (with one space left for a 'door').

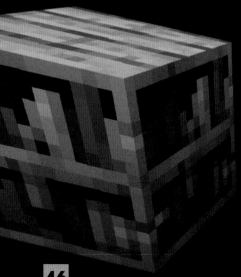

CHOOSE YOUR WEAPON

Even if you've only got one or two bookshelves up, it's still worth using the enchantment table, as the only cost involved is experience points, which you can lose at any time anyway! Of course, you'll want to choose your best armour or prime weapons and tools to upgrade, but it can pay to have a few of each, as different enchantments are useful in different situations – and you still have to live with durability issues, which makes the Mending enchantment a good choice for any item.

TIP!
You can also use an anvil to combine enchanted items or use any enchanted books you find or craft to boost your gear.

YOU'RE A WIZARD!

To apply an enchantment, use the table and place the item in the first slot. In the second slot you'll need to place some lapis lazuli (the blue stuff you'll find when mining). This will then offer up three options for you to choose from, each requiring a certain XP level, so just make your choice and take your new-and-improved item! You can't specify what you want in advance, so it might take a few tries to get the best options, but you can remove enchantments on a grindstone and try again.

REPAIR AND COMBINE

Don't use the crafting table to repair these items as it will remove any enchantments. Instead, you'll need to use an anvil, along with the source material (and a little XP). You can also use the anvil to combine two enchanted items into one, with the fixed item absorbing the other's durability. Plus there's a good chance of inheriting its enchantment as well which can help you add several upgrades to a single piece of kit!

TIP!
You can place a book into the first slot to create an enchanted book and 'save' the power to your storage to apply to your gear later using an anvil.

TEN OF THE BEST ENCHANTMENTS

Efficiency – mine up to five times faster.

Feather Falling – reduces the damage you take from falling.

Frost Walker – add to boots to turn water to ice so you can walk on it.

Infinity – turns one normal arrow into an infinite supply.

Looting – increases the chance of mobs dropping rare resources.

Luck of the Sea – add to a fishing rod to catch better loot.

Mending – repairs durability every time you collect experience orbs.

Protection – reduces the amount of damage you take.

Sharpness – increases the damage of melee weapons.

Silk Touch – when you mine one resource you might get a whole block (x64!).

The Craft-y Quiz

Hopefully you've learned a few things from these pages, but let's really put your Minecraft knowledge to the test.

No cheating!

01

Which of the following is NOT the name of a lead character in Minecraft?

a) Alex
b) Kim
c) Steve

02

In terms of base damage, what's the best melee weapon after the sword?

a) Axe
b) Pickaxe
c) Shovel

03

Which of these blocks can't be left suspended in mid-air?

a) Dirt
b) Granite
c) Gravel

04

If you need a hunger and health boost, what is probably best avoided?

a) Bread
b) Cooked porkchop
c) Rotten flesh

05

The Caves & Cliffs update added the game's first amphibian. What is it?

a) Axolotl
b) Newt
c) Salamander

06

What's the favourite food of cows and sheep?

a) Carrots
b) Seeds
c) Wheat

07

In the Overworld, in what direction would your compass point?

a) Due North
b) Towards your latest bed
c) Towards your spawn point

08

There are three special types of rail, besides the standard tracks, activator, powered and...?

a) Booster
b) Detector
c) Leaf-covered

09

What's the key component in any powered circuit?

a) Glowstone
b) Lapis lazuli
c) Redstone

10

What's the name of the enchantment that turns water to ice when you step on it?

a) Cool Runnings
b) Frost Walker
c) Ice Skater

11

When you're building a Nether portal, what block should you use?

a) Blackstone
b) Obsidian
c) Soul sand

12

What do Piglins love?

a) Cheesy puffs
b) Diamonds
c) Gold

13

The ender dragon can heal itself using what?

a) End crystals
b) Fire charges
c) Nether quartz

14

If you're looking to fire up the End portal, what should you be crafting?

a) 12 eyes of ender
b) 5 gold rings
c) Partridge in a pear tree

15

What's the name of the super-tough underground mob introduced in the Wild update?

a) The warden
b) The watcher
c) The witcher

16

What will happen if you place a bed in the Nether?

a) Creepy nightmares
b) It explodes
c) You get a lie-in

17

If you're hit with a Status effect, what can you consume to cure yourself?

a) Cake
b) Cookies
c) Milk

18

What do you need to 'fly' in Survival Mode?

a) Elytra
b) Golden apple
c) Super saddle

19

Endermen are creepy on a good day, but what don't they like you doing?

a) Mining gold
b) Staring at them
c) Telling bad jokes

20

And finally, when it comes to weapons and armour, what's the toughest material in the game?

a) Alwaysrite
b) Netherite
c) Neverite

To find out how you got on, turn to page 78 for the answers!

MODEL VILLAGE

Villages will appear in many of the major biomes, populated with villagers who can take on a number of roles within the community. They're completely harmless unless you attack them, but you might want to check they don't have an iron golem for protection first! If you play nice, you'll be able to trade freely with many of the local residents and pick up a number of useful resources that could save you a lot of mining time!

TIP!

If your local village doesn't have a trader who specialises in what you might need, placing the relevant crafting table can encourage an unemployed villager to take on the role!

Trading
WITH
Villagers

How you can turn a quaint little village into a thriving resource of invaluable items!

WORKING FROM HOME

There are some 15 different roles a villager can take on, including unemployed and nitwit (the village idiot!). Some of the more familiar ones you'll want to be dealing with include clerics, farmers, librarians and the toolsmith. Basically, every type of crafting block you can make (brewing stand, cartography table, smithing table and so on) comes with a job relating to it, and they should give you a good idea about the kind of items that they'll have to trade. You'll soon learn to recognise each profession's signature look!

Level 1 – Novice
Level 2 – Apprentice
Level 1 – Farmer
Trade ?
Inventory

MAKING A TRADE

Interact with a villager to open up the trading interface. You'll likely have a couple of possible trades open to you, as long as you have the required items, with others that are locked out. Simply choose the deal that appeals to you and the trade will be made. Early on the trades might not seem very favourable, such as several emeralds for an otherwise basic resource, but it can pay in the long run to make the sacrifice to access better loot later on.

LEVELLING UP

The reason you'll want to make several trades with the same person is because the villagers also have experience levels. With most deals you'll see their level increase, building from a level 1 novice, up to a level 2 apprentice, and ultimately to a level 5 master. Each level brings new and rarer items, without too much of a 'price' increase, which can save you a lot of hunting around for valuable resources. Villagers can run out of goods, requiring a 'restock' cooldown period, while the prices can also vary depending on demand and supply.

TRASH TO TREASURE

You can look to turn some of your unwanted inventory items into a trade with random villagers by holding what you want to sell in your hand and walking around the town. Anyone interested in what you're offering will similarly hold up whatever item they'd be willing to swap for it. You can then approach them to open up the trade menu and see if the numbers are something you're happy to deal with.

TIP!
You can earn bonus rewards and discounts by defending the settlement from a pillager raid (which you can invoke with a Bad Omen status effect!), earning yourself the title of 'Hero of the Village'.

TRADING WITH PIGLINS

Make a few friends in the Nether and you might be able to snag some rare loot drops!

PRECIOUS PIGLINS

Piglins are a common mob found across the Nether, and they can be a tough enemy that can attack in number. However, they also have a love of gold that you can take advantage of, initially by wearing a single piece of gold armour which will stop them from attacking you. It will lower your protection compared to iron or diamond, but the reduced threat makes it worthwhile. A gold chestpiece looks cool but a helmet is the cheaper option!

GOLDEN NUGGETS

You'll quickly notice that the Nether has a decent supply of gold blocks for mining. Unlike the Overworld, these offer up gold nuggets, that you'll need to craft (not smelt) into gold ingots. Just keep an eye out for piglins as they can take offence if they see you mining gold or opening up loot chests, and may attack even if you are wearing some gold armour.

MAKE THE DROP

Once you've got a good supply of gold ingots (and that gold armour!), you should be able to find some now-friendly neighbourhood adult piglins in all Nether biomes. All you have to do to initiate a trade is to drop a gold ingot onto the ground between you. The piglin should pick it up and spend a few seconds basking in its beauty. After a short delay, they'll pocket the ingot and throw out an item of their own onto the floor for you to pick up.

TIP!
If gold is in short supply, don't forget you can head back through the portal at any time to bring some back from your Overworld mining!

TAKE YOUR REWARD

Unlike trading with villagers, you don't get a choice of what you get in return. Instead, the piglin will drop a random item from a shortlist within its inventory. As you might expect, many items are linked to the Nether, and include fire resistance potions and enchanted books. Crucially for your Survival mode progress, they can also throw out ender pearls and soul sand, which you'll need to reach the End and spawn the wither – meaning a little bit of gold spent on piglins could save you a lot of time on your ultimate quest!

TIP!
Baby piglins will take your gold but won't give anything back, so be sure to only trade with adults!

53

GEAR UP FOR AN EPIC ADVENTURE!

If you're never really sure about what to do next in Minecraft, why not set yourself the challenge of beating the game? Here's everything you need to do it.

TIP!
Playing the game on Peaceful can make things a LOT easier, but you'll need to be on at least Easy to spawn the enemies you'll need to defeat. Of course, beating it on Hard is the ultimate challenge!

TIP!
Speed-running Minecraft is a popular side-dish to the game – how quickly can you get from that first spawn point to the end of, well, the End?

Survival mode is a truly epic adventure for Minecrafters. Whether you end up scaling the highest mountains, reaching the deepest, darkest caves, or even transporting to a whole new dimension, you'll face some of the game's toughest challenges – and all while never really knowing what might be coming next.

You'll start with nothing and have to search, scavenge and mine your way to becoming the toughest kid in town, while mastering some of the coolest kit to be able to take down some huge boss battles! There are no missions or quests, and it's not something that you'll be able to complete in a hurry, but by breaking Survival mode down into smaller and more manageable chunks, it's actually a lot easier to beat than you might think.

With every small step you take comes some better gear, or you'll learn a fresh trick, or figure out how some new crafting item works, and in turn those will make the next step that much easier to complete. It can be a long and dangerous road, but over the following pages we'll lay out everything you need to know, and do, to find yourself standing toe-to-toe with the ender dragon ready to claim the title of 'Minecraft Superstar'!

All you need to do to get started is punch a tree...

GOOD LUCK!

SURVIVAL MODE CHECKLIST

This isn't everything you'll need to do, but they're all big steps – so every time you tick something off give yourself a prize!

OVERWORLD

- [ ] Punched a tree!
- [ ] Survived the first day
- [ ] Built your first home
- [ ] Mined for coal and iron
- [ ] Upgraded your tools
- [ ] Found obsidian for Nether portal

THE NETHER

- [ ] Reached the Nether
- [ ] Built a base around the Nether portal
- [ ] Found soul sand and wither skulls
- [ ] Upgraded/enchanted your weapons
- [ ] Summoned and beat the wither

THE END

- [ ] Collected blaze rods and ender pearls
- [ ] Crafted (at least) 12 eyes of ender
- [ ] Found the stronghold
- [ ] Built the End portal
- [ ] Seriously upgraded EVERYTHING
- [ ] Entered the End
- [ ] Defeated the ender dragon
- [ ] Attained awesomeness!

TIP!
When creating your game, toggle the 'bonus chest' slider to give yourself some handy start-up items!

X Crafting

Y Inventory

SURVIVING THE FIRST NIGHT

Your first day in Minecraft can be the toughest, as you start empty handed with barely 10 minutes until the light begins to fade and hostile mobs start to spawn. Here's what you need to do so make it safely through to the morning.

Crafting

Inventory

RT Mine

1 PUNCH A TREE

With the exception of an empty map, you start in Survival mode with nothing in your inventory, so your first task is to craft some tools. To get the basics you need just head straight for the nearest tree and mine it with your empty hand to start gathering the wood that drops. In some biomes, such as snowy mountains or a barren desert, trees can be pretty scarce, and having lots of wood nearby can make these early days a lot easier!

TIP! If trees are in short supply, mine their leaves to drop saplings, then plant these to grow some more!

2 GET CRAFTING

After mining a couple of trees, open up the crafting panel. You'll see your initial options are very limited, but for now you just need to use the wood to create wooden planks, and then use those to make some sticks. These are basic building materials used throughout the game so feel free to stock up when you've got a bit more time! You can use some of those planks to build a crafting table. Placing this anywhere will give you access to more crafting options (you can mine the table to pick it up again).

MAKE SOME TOOLS

You're now ready to make your first set of tools! If you've got easy access to punch a few cobblestone blocks, you can jump straight to stone, but we'll use wood to get you started. Craft the wooden pickaxe, axe, shovel and sword – the others can wait for a little while. Those wooden tools won't last for long, so you might want to make a few spares if you've got the supplies! Don't forget to move at least one of each into the bottom row of your inventory so you've got quick access to them.

BUILD A SHELTER: THE QUICK FIX

You don't have time to look around for a prime location to start building, as night isn't far off and you'll be very vulnerable to enemies at this point. One quick and simple solution is to just dig a hole into the side of a hill or mountain, or even just in the ground nearby. It can be as small as 2x3 blocks in size (and 2 blocks tall) and all you have to do is block up the entrance behind you to keep any mobs at bay and you'll be safe until dawn! Though you might want to leave at least a one-block hole to let some light in, as waiting in the dark can be a bit creepy.

BUILD A SHELTER: YOUR FIRST HOUSE

Although you don't have time to make anything too large or stylish, you can quickly mine some dirt or cobblestone and use it to build a simple starter home. Something around 6x4 blocks in size and 3-4 blocks tall (including the walls and ceiling) is plenty to house all you need to get started. You can then either build a door or place a dirt block in the gap behind you to keep the mobs from getting in and you're all set. You can leave one block spaces for windows, but be wary of skeletons firing arrows through the gaps!

WAIT UNTIL SUNRISE

The night cycle lasts for seven minutes in total, but you can use this time at your crafting table to top up your inventory, perhaps adding a chest to store any spare items, or torches if you were lucky enough to find coal nearby. When the sun comes up, undead enemies will catch fire and die when in direct sunlight, while any others will seek darkness underground, so wait until the coast is clear (or chase down any remaining enemies with your sword!) and you'll be free to embrace the new day.

> **TIP!** Placing a second chest directly next to another one, combines them into one single large chest to save you swapping between them.

START MINING

We've already covered the basics to mining, so if there isn't a convenient cave nearby to look in, it's time to get out the pickaxe! You don't need to dig too deep for now, as early on you only really need to be finding coal to help make torches and fuel your furnace, and raw iron that you can smelt in the furnace to create iron ingots. With these ingots you can make your toolset stronger with iron gear, and maybe even craft your first pieces of armour as well.

MINE AND CRAFT!

Once you've made it safely through the night, the temptation is to head straight out and explore. However, there are a few things you might want to do before heading out into the unknown.

FIND SOME FOOD

You don't have to eat loads in Minecraft, but it can be really important for replenishing any lost health. Hunting the local animals to get raw meat to cook in your furnace is an easy option, or you can look around for trees and bushes that have a good supply of apples or berries. If you're expanding your home, you can also think about starting up a small farm area to grow basic crops, such as wheat, and start playing around with some home cooking.

EXPAND YOUR HOME

Although it might not become your main base of operations, it's worth creating a bit more space in your starter home to craft and place a few more useful items. You'll need a furnace to cook food and smelt raw metals from your mining, plus a bed, and it can also be handy to place an extra chest or two so you can split up your resources and make things easier to find. If you're still dealing in dirt or cobblestone, it shouldn't take too long to just knock down a wall and extend it out a few blocks.

FURNACE

> **TIP!**
> If creepers keep blowing up your hard work, build a perimeter wall a few blocks out to keep them at a safe distance.

MAKE A BED

Beds are important because they act as your respawn point. If you die without a bed, you'll keep returning to your original spawn point - which can sometimes be a long trip back! Plus, sleeping in a bed will fast-forward time through the night, which can save a lot of trouble with those annoying mobs. To make one you'll need 3x wool of the same colour and 3x wooden planks, so you might want to start looking around for some sheep!

SHEEP

> **TIP!**
> You can get wool without harming sheep by equipping some shears. Plus, you'll get more wool than you would by just killing them.

GO FISH!

This is more a fun optional extra but, if you spawn near water, it's pretty easy to hook up a rod and catch some fish. You'll probably need to kill a spider or two to get some string to craft it, but then you can just equip the fishing rod like any other tool and 'mine' the sea. Just cast the line and watch for the tell-tale bubbles of an incoming bite. As your lure drops, hit the mine button again to instantly reel in your catch. There's a lot of fish that make for a good snack when cooked (and cats love raw cod and salmon!), but you can also find some other very handy items beneath the waves, including enchantments for your gear.

THERE'S SOME GOOD LOOT UNDER THE WAVES!

Build a Home Base

Making your first home can be a Creative-style big-build, or you can keep things rather more practical. Here are some solid foundations to get you started.

SCOUT AROUND

You might not want to stray too far but it's worth having a good look around for a prime location for your new base of operations. Finding some high ground can be a great way to spot large open areas, or distant caves and biomes that you might want to explore. Ideally, you'll be able to find a spot with lots of space to build and expand into, or you can just dig straight into a mountain for an underground lair!

BUILD A HOME

TIP!
You don't need to find a large open place to get started, as you can always mine an area to clear a good location into a prime building spot!

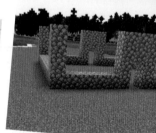
FOUNDATIONS

SCOUT AROUND

BUILDING BLOCKS

Start by laying the foundations just one block high until you're happy with the size and shape — not forgetting spaces for doors! As you build upwards, you can place sand in the furnace to make glass for your windows (or as a nice skylight) and set aside space for chests, crafting items and so on. As for what building materials to use, that might depend on where you spawn — for example, a forest will give you enough materials for a cool wooden cabin — but there'll always be plenty of cobblestone around, making a castle a good go-to design style to start with!

STARTER MINE?

THINK BIG

Your home doesn't need to be huge, but it can be useful to add at least one extra floor. Having some space upstairs, or digging out a basement below, can give you somewhere to place important items a safe distance from exploding creepers! Adding a balcony or roof area can also give you a safe spot to pick off distant enemies with a crossbow.

TIP!
Place your bed on an upper floor, as this will increase the distance from any mobs outside that can stop you from sleeping through the night.

BEDROOM

FINISHING TOUCHES

Quite how 'homely' you want to make it is up to you. However, as well as using torches inside to keep it well lit at night, a good number of light sources placed outside your house will also make it a lot easier to spot from far away when you're exploring.

PAINTINGS

BUILD YOUR OWN HOME!

If you're more of a builder than a miner, one fun Creative project is to recreate your own home. In Minecraft, one block equals one square metre in the real world, so grab a tape measure and make a scale version of your house! It's also a good way to play with some of the many tools and mechanics to try and recreate items in your home that you might not find ready-made in the game..

COOL POOL

TIP!
Have fun with your surroundings. Find a small pool of water? Style it out into your own outdoor swimming pool!

WINDOWS

LIGHT IT UP!

REACHING THE NETHER

TIP!
For a better chance of creating obsidian, mine a path for water to flow into a lava pool. If lava flows into water it will create a cobblestone block instead.

When you're ready to take the first big step into beating Survival mode, it's time to open a portal to the Nether.

BE PREPARED!

The Nether is a hostile place with some tough and hostile enemies, with lots of ways to catch fire and no water around to cool you down, so it's not something to rush into until you're comfortable in combat. As well as a good sword, a bow or crossbow for ranged combat is a good idea as some enemies will keep their distance. Armour is also recommended, with at least one piece of gold armour enough to stop piglins from attacking.

As well as a good supply of food, you might also want to consider packing a fishing rod, as it can be used to find warped fungus in lava pools. This can then be combined with stick to help steer striders, which you can ride by equipping a saddle and even walk across lava. Enhancements can be a big help, especially the likes of Fire Protection for obvious reasons, while Frost Walker will also let you walk across magma blocks without taking damage for some handy shortcuts!

TIP!
If you're a few obsidian blocks short, you can leave out the four corner pieces or just use another block type, reducing the total count from 14 to 10.

TAKE SUPPLIES

You won't want to be stuck for a back-up weapon or crafting table, so make sure you've got everything you might need, which might include iron and wood for new tools as they can be hard to find in the Nether. Don't take anything that you don't need as you'll want to save inventory slots for any good loot you find. Similarly, don't take something that you can't afford to lose until you've got a replacement back at your base. Also pack some torches or some other way to help you track a path back to the portal when it's time to leave!

MINE OBSIDIAN

To build the portal, you'll need at least 10 blocks of obsidian. This is formed where water meets lava, so the chances are you'll need to find some lava pools deep underground. To mine it you'll need to craft a diamond pickaxe, but the good news is that diamonds can often be found in good supply in areas where obsidian can form. With a good coming together of water and lava, you should be able to farm plenty of obsidian from a single location with which to build your portal.

BUILD THE PORTAL

You'll need to build a portal in the Overworld. This is a vertical frame of obsidian blocks that must be at least four blocks wide and five blocks high (up to a maximum of 23x23), leaving at least a 2x3 'hole' in the middle. There's no limit as to where you can build it, but obviously it's something you may be using a lot, so you'll want it to be near a main base or some other favoured spawn point.

JUMP IN!

Once the portal is built you'll need to light it. The easiest way is with a flint and steel, but anything that will start a fire should do it. Once lit, it will burn with a bright purple light that you can now jump into, although you might need to stand still for a second or two for the teleportation to take effect. When it does, a corresponding portal will be automatically dropped into the Nether to establish your link between the two worlds – so if you don't like what you see be ready to turn around and jump back to the Overworld!

THE NETHER: HOT TIPS

The Nether can be an intimidating place but with a few smarts and a little patience, you'll be prepped and ready to explore this strange new world.

PORTAL PROTECTION

1 Your portal can be destroyed, so your first job should be to build a wall or even a base around it to prevent it from taking any damage. A fire-proof cobblestone shelter is a quick and easy option, and will also protect you against ghast fireballs.

2 You can make endless return journeys, so don't be afraid to jump back and forth to stay out of trouble or recover when setting up your first base around the portal.

3 Those ghasts can be annoying, but they won't follow you and will only fire when you're in their line of sight. Plus, they can't see through glass, which can work to your advantage as you can take them out with a couple of arrows fired from a safe spot.

4 There are five main biomes – crimson forest, warped forest, basalt deltas, soul sand valley and Nether wastes. Each come with their own unique enemies and items, plus a variety of blocks that you'll only find in the Nether. The world's overall size may vary depending on the version of the game you're playing.

AVOID FIREBALLS!

VERY WILD-LIFE!

5 It has no day-night cycle, with the downside being that this means enemies are pretty much a constant threat. Fortunately, the tough zombified piglins will leave you alone unless you attack them.

6 Fortunately, it's not all that dark, with a natural ambient light level equal to around 8 in the Overworld, but you'll still want to pack some torches!

7 However, there's no water here, which can be a problem because lava and fire is common, so be super-careful when mining and always have a safe place to back out to in case you dig into a hot spot!

8 One block in the Nether equals eight blocks in the Overworld, which can make it a great fast travel system once you've established some safe areas with extra portals.

9 It can be a good idea to take 10 blocks of obsidian and a flint and steel on your travels, so if you do get lost or need an escape route you've got a quick way back to the Overworld that doesn't involve dying.

10 Beds explode in the Nether, so be prepared to go a long time without any sleep. You'll need to place a charged respawn anchor to act as your respawn point if you die, otherwise you'll be returned to the Overworld.

11 Compasses are useless here unless you connect them to a lodestone – which the compass will then point towards, so it can pay to have one near your portal.

A WARM WELCOME

12 The castle-like Nether fortresses are the best places to find blazes and wither skeletons, which you'll have to kill to gain the resources needed to reach the End.

13 Bastion remnants are mean-looking fortifications that will have a lot of enemies to navigate but offers lots of great rewards, including gold blocks and loot chests.

BEATING THE WITHER

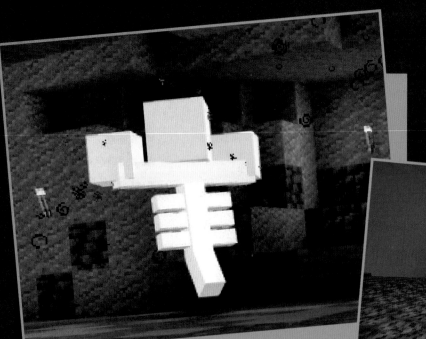

The game's first boss battle won't be easy, but you can tilt the odds in your favour.

WHAT YOU'LL NEED

To get the wither to spawn, you'll need three wither skulls and four blocks of soul sand (or soul soil) found in soul sand valleys. You'll get the skulls by killing wither skeletons who spawn in Nether fortresses – though the drop chance is low, so a Looting enhancement can boost your chances but it may still take a while. One very difficult trick is to get a charged creeper to kill them during a storm for a guaranteed skull drop!

CHOOSE YOUR BATTLEGROUND

The good news is that the wither can spawn in any dimension and always in a place of your choosing, so you can head back to the Overworld and fight it on your own turf. It might be tempting, but you don't want to be too close to your base or anything else that could get destroyed, as the wither can smash its way through most block types during your battle, so you don't want to risk losing anything valuable!

PLAN AHEAD

Before starting you might want to put up some blocks or mine a few areas to give you some hiding spots to recover or a safe house for supplies, with obsidian being a tough, but not completely unbreakable option if you've got some to spare. You can even get creative and build some traps or narrow tunnels the wither is too big to fit into to give you an advantage when the battle begins.

BE PREPARED

You should also make sure you're fully stocked up with weapons and your best recovery foods. Of course, enchanted armour and weapons, as well as some choice potions can make things a lot easier, so be sure to take your very best loadout into battle! When you're ready, place the sand into an upright 'T' shape. Add the three skulls on top, but only place the third when you're absolutely ready, as that will cause the wither to appear.

TIP!
Among many different tricks to make the fight easier, you can try using mobs to your advantage, with iron golems, endermen and even bees proving useful allies!

KEEP YOUR DISTANCE

The wither will charge up into an explosive blast upon arrival, so back up to avoid taking early damage. You'll want to keep your distance at the beginning, too, so focus on your bow or crossbow with fully-charged ranged attacks. The wither's attack patterns and difficulty can vary depending on the version of the game you're playing, but you'll need to avoid being hit directly by its skulls and stay patient until it comes into range. When it drops to half health, your bow will no longer hurt it, so look to get in closer and use your sword to deliver some critical hits to finish it off quickly.

GRAB THAT NETHER STAR!

As a parting shot, the wither will once again charge up and explode, so make sure you back up once again to avoid being caught in the blast. Now that it's most definitely dead, it will drop a Nether star, which you can take back to your Overworld base and use to build a beacon as a shining showcase of your wither-killing skills. More on that in a few pages time.

TIP!
Underground can make for a good location as a cave area can stop the wither flying away, while offering lots of places you can use as recovery or hiding spots.

HOW TO THE REACH THE END

Finding the End portal is half of the battle of completing this surreal otherworld.

THE BEGINNING OF THE END

A strange void-like suspended inter-dimension, the End somehow manages to be even less hospitable than the Nether, due to its limited resources and the huge distances you may have to travel to discover its secrets. The good news is, you only really need to win one boss battle to complete the game (or at least reach the end credits sequence), which is triggered almost as soon as you arrive there. The very bad news is that the boss fight can be incredibly tough, and the trek to get there is only slightly easier, but it can be much, much longer...

WHAT YOU'LL NEED

To open the End portal you'll need up to 12 eyes of ender, with the amount varying depending on the version of the game you're playing and how lucky you get! These are crafted using blaze dust – made from rods that drop from fallen blazes in the Nether – and the ender pearls you can get from killing endermen. You can also find, and trade for, all of these elements on your travels, and carrying more than 12 can be recommended as they also help you find your way to the End.

FINDING THE PORTAL

The portal will be buried deep underground within a stronghold somewhere in the Overworld. It's needle-in-a-haystack-of-needles territory if you go hunting blind, but thankfully the eyes of ender are drawn towards it. To get a bearing, simply throw an eye into the air with the 'use' button. It will drift away in the direction of the portal for up to 12 blocks, leaving a purple trail behind it pointing the way. After each use it will drop to the ground, so be sure not to throw it up over lava or anywhere else you won't be able to recover it!

ACCESSING THE STRONGHOLD

Bearing in mind you could be thousands of blocks away, you'll most likely be in for a very long trip (and risk losing a few eyes on the way), so you may well need to make some stop-off bases to rest and resupply along the way. When you get close, the thrown eyes will begin zooming down towards a spot on the ground. This is the time to start digging to reach the stronghold hidden below! Once inside search around its labyrinth of tunnels (with its many enemies to fight and chests to loot) until you find a mysterious device suspended over a lava pit.

USING THE PORTAL

Thankfully this is the easy bit. You just need to place an eye of ender into each of the available spaces – if you're lucky one or two will already be installed (if you're REALLY lucky, they all will be). With all spots taken, the central area will transform into a black void portal that you can jump into to reach the End. Before you do, though, you'll want to set up a nearby camp, complete with a bed to respawn in, because initially the End is a one-way trip and the only way out is if you die or successfully defeat the ender dragon – so make sure you're absolutely ready for the fight before you head inside.

TIP!
Blazes are highly vulnerable to snowballs, so what may have seemed like nothing more than a fun distraction in a snowy biome, can be very useful in the Nether!

TIP!
The eyes of ender will rise up at a steeper angle the further you are away from the stronghold, so you can get a sense of how close (or not!) you are.

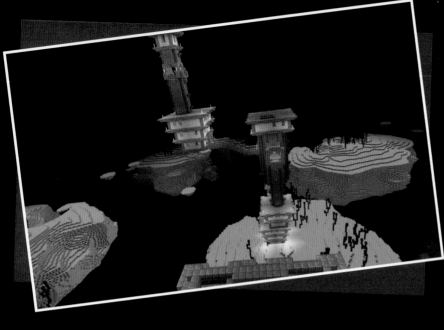

EXPERT TIPS FOR LIFE IN THE END

The End is a strange and largely barren land. There's little need for mining, but a few long trips can bring some great rewards. Here's your local travel guide.

1 After defeating the ender dragon, a smaller second 'gateway' portal will appear leading to the outer islands. You can throw an ender pearl at it to enter and be randomly teleported, with every subsequent portal you find bringing you back to this original location.

GATEWAY PORTAL

2 You can respawn the ender dragon at any time, by placing an End crystal on the middle block of each of the four sides of the exit portal (opposite each of the four torches on the central pillar).

EXIT PORTAL

3 Despite looking largely alike, in the Java Edition of the game, the End is split into five biomes: the End, small End islands, End midlands, End highlands and End barrens.

4 The music in the End sounds weird and creepy, but it's just a distorted version of the normal soundtrack. See if you can recognise any of the tracks!

5 As with the Nether, there's no day-night cycle, beds will explode, and compasses won't work unless you place a lodestone – which can be useful for finding your way back to a gateway portal.

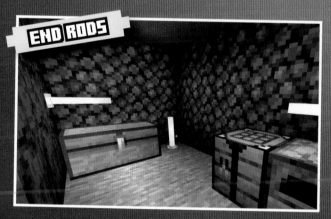

END RODS

6 You can also use the chorus fruit in the furnace to get a 'popped' variant. It isn't edible but it can be combined with blaze rods to craft End rods as a stylish light source.

7 Unlike the Nether, you can't use a respawn anchor here either, which is why it's a good idea to place a bed near the End portal in the Overworld for a quick return in case you die.

8 Appropriately, the End is filled with endermen which can make it tricky to navigate peacefully, but if you craft and equip a pumpkin hat, they'll leave you alone.

9 You can mine the purple chorus plants for a near endless supply of food – but be careful as eating their chorus fruit will randomly teleport you a few blocks, so make sure there's no risk of dropping into the void!

10 The End cities are more like towers, that usually require some careful platforming to climb up, with shulkers protecting the loot chests at the top.

END CITY

11 Shulkers will drop shulker shells that can be crafted into shulker boxes. These are chests that keep all items inside when you break it, meaning you can carry a fully-stocked box in a single inventory slot to seriously boost your carrying capacity.

12 To defeat shulkers, you'll want to arm yourself with a shield to block their projectile attacks, which can otherwise follow you around and knock you off the ground.

ENDER CHEST

13 In End cities you can also find ender chests. These are like cloud storage for your goods, as all chests will share the same placed items and each is unique to the player – so in multiplayer no-one else can grab your stash!

DEFEATING THE ENDER DRAGON

Just one more battle separates you from Minecraft glory, and you'll need to take your best game to the End to bring home the ultimate prize.

THE ENDER DAYS

It should come as no surprise to hear that the ender dragon is one tough enemy. Not only does it have a fiery breath that leaves a toxic smoke in its wake, but it also blasts out fireballs that can make a mess of your health bar and the world around you. This is a fight of tactics and patience, and you're going to need your very best gear to come out on top.

BE PREPARED

Visiting the End for the first time almost immediately triggers the ender dragon encounter, so don't use the End portal until you're 100% ready. You'll want to equip your best armour and weapons, including a powerful ranged option, while a good mix of enchantments and potions can go a long way. A large number of healing items can help on top of your favourite foods, while any spare obsidian can also be useful as the ender dragon can't destroy those blocks, so building some quick defences can save you a lot of damage.

TIP!
Building a 'lift' by jumping up and placing a block under your feet is a quick trick to get to the top of these pillars – then just mine yourself back down to ground level.

TIP!
If you're feeling brave, you can take a break from the fight to bottle up some of the purple smoke. This 'dragon's breath' can be used to make Lingering potions.

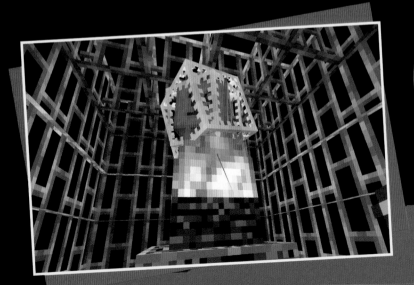

AIM HIGH

When the ender dragon first appears, you'll see it circling around some tall obsidian pillars. On top of these are End crystals, which it can use to heal – and at a rate higher than the damage you'll likely be able to dish out. This means your first step is to destroy as many of them as you can. You can use ranged weapons, or build a quick route up to smash the crystal with a single hit. Once they're all gone you can turn your attention to the main event.

THIS MIGHT DRAG-ON

To defeat the ender dragon you can use an enchanted bow to chip away at its health from afar, using the obsidian pillars or your own built defences to act as cover and a safe place to recover. It will combine its fiery blasts with swooping attacks, so make sure you steer clear of it's primary moves and counter with quick shots of your own (headshots do a lot more damage!).

It can also perch on the smaller central pillar – which is actually your exit portal – where you can move in for some quick hits with your sword. Be patient and don't push your luck, and though it may take some time you should eventually land the fatal blow.

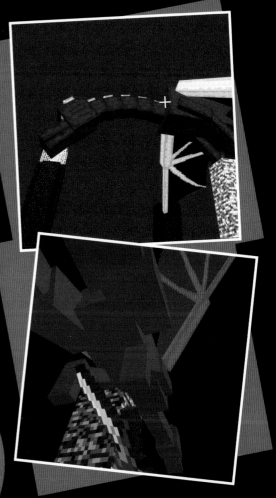

TIP!
Upon its death, the ender dragon will also spawn a dragon egg on the exit portal. It can't be used for anything, but it can make for a cool trophy of awesomeness to put on display in your base!

THE END CREDITS

As with the wither, the ender dragon dies in a powerful explosion, so make sure you're not anywhere close when that happens. Its death will open up the exit portal which you can jump into to head back to your last respawn point and continue your adventure.

However, before that you get to enjoy a long, whimsical and occasionally silly 'poem' that leads into the game's seemingly endless credits. You can skip it, but maybe take a moment to sit back, take a breath and bask in the glory of what you've just done – you've beaten Survival mode!
You. Are. Awesome!

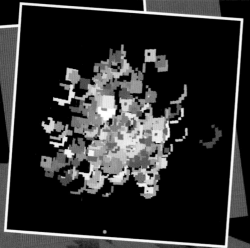

TIP!
The materials used to build the pyramid have no impact on the beacon's effect, so while diamond may look great, iron will work just as well.

BUILD A BEACON

Nothing shouts 'I've killed the wither' more than using its Nether star to build yourself a base-buffing light to the stars.

BEACON BUDDY
Not only does the beacon provide a vertical beam of light that anyone else in your game will be able to see from miles away as a clear sign of your Minecraft greatness, but they also give powerful buffs to you and any other players within its radius. Plus, they look pretty cool and with the Nether star you collect for beating the wither not being of use for anything else, why not build one? Of course, if you'd rather your base remains a little more secretive, then a beacon might not be the best idea.

WHAT YOU'LL NEED

To build the beacon, you'll need to craft it by combining the Nether star with four blocks of glass and three of obsidian. This acts as the top of what could become a multi-layered pyramid. The power of the beacon's effects increases with each level you build, up to a maximum of four levels. These levels need to be made from blocks of iron, gold, diamond, emerald and/or netherite. You can mix and match them however you like!

A TALL ORDER

Depending on how big you want (or can afford) your pyramid to be, you'll need to figure out how big your base layer needs to be. You'll need a 3x3 square for the top, 5x5 for the second layer, 7x7 for the third and a 9x9 grid at the bottom for the biggest beacon. This means that for the four options, you'll need to have a combined total of 9, 36, 83 and 164 blocks. That's not a problem in Creative mode with limitless supplies, but in Survival mode that's a lot of mining!

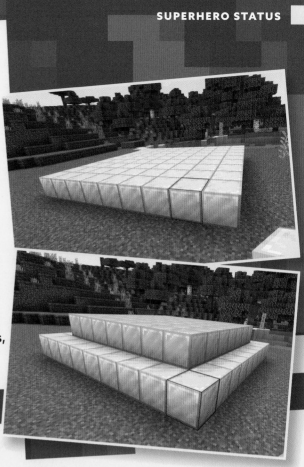

BUILDING BLOCKS

Putting the pyramid together is pretty easy. Just place the required number of blocks in a square for your first layer, and then drop the gradually decreasing-sized layers on top. As with most Minecraft items, you can mine all of these elements to get the resources back, so you can disassemble and rebuild your pyramid with extra blocks if you need to start small and build it up over time. With your pyramid ready, place the beacon in the centre block of the 3x3 layer and it will burst into life!

CHOOSE YOUR POWERS

Your beacon offers a choice of up to five primary powers, depending on the height of your pyramid, plus a single secondary health boost. Your options, in the order they appear with each layer, are Speed, Haste (faster mining), Resistance, Jump Boost and Strength (for more damage). You just need to make your choice, hit the tick, and you'll see some bubbles popping up to confirm they've taken effect. You'll see their two fixed icons appear on your screen whenever you're in range – which will flash when you start heading too far out before disappearing.

Of course, there's nothing to stop you from taking on the wither again and again, and building yourself a second beacon, or even a fifth one to cover all of the power-ups if you really want to show off.

TIP!

You can change the colour of the beam of light, by placing a stained-glass block on top of the beacon.

FLYING WITH THE ELYTRA

Your reward for fully exploring the End is the ability to 'fly' in Survival mode.

Okay, it's not really flying, more a case of falling with style, with the elytra working like a wingsuit which you can use to glide gracefully from any height. It works in a similar way to flying in Creative mode, but you're on a more constant downward-trajectory with gravity doing its thing. You will be able to 'fly' upwards but you'll need to show a little more control...

WHERE TO FIND IT

You can't craft the elytra; you can only find it in the End after you've defeated the ender dragon. This will open up a small gateway portal to the outer islands for you to explore. You don't need to mine anything, but you might have to travel great distances to find the End cities or ships that will dominate the landscape. You'll find the elytra mounted on a wall inside the treasure room of an End ship. Take care to navigate the nearby shulkers protecting the loot and you'll be ready to make good use of your new flying friend.

EQUIPPING THE ELYTRA

To use it, you just need to place it into your chestpiece armour slot – which will reduce your protection level, so only do so when you need it. With the elytra equipped, any time you're falling you can press the jump button to spring it into life, so finding a nice tall mountain would be a great starting point. Plus, it's a handy escape tool if you happen to accidentally tumble off the ledge of a deep cavern!

TIP!
You can make a quick take-off point anywhere by building a tower of blocks under your feet. Just jump and place until you're high enough!

SEA VIEW

FAST TRAVEL

FLYING HIGH

In the air, you can steer the elytra by using the camera controls to bank and turn. Heading towards the ground will give you a speed boost, while you can slow and gain some altitude by looking up – with fireworks being a neat trick to give you a speed boost! Be careful, though, because if you push too steeply upwards the elytra can stall, which can send you into spin, requiring some quick corrections to put you back into control. You can make a smooth landing by coming in at a narrow angle, or use the jump button to end the flight when you're happy you can survive the drop.

GLIDING HOME

FALLING WITH STYLE!

USE IT WISELY

As tempting as it is to swoop around the skies for ages, the elytra has a durability that means it will stop working when it runs out (though it never breaks). You get less than 10 minutes of use, so you don't want to run out of juice mid-flight! You can repair it by combining it with a second elytra on a grindstone or with phantom membranes using the anvil. The price can go up with each subsequent fix, but you can reset this by removing an enchantment on the grindstone. This can make it a costly item to use, but if you need to cover large distances in a hurry, there's no better way to travel!

TIP!
The Mending enhancement can be great for the elytra, repairing its durability every time you kill another mob.

Answers

Page 16 - Messed Up Mobs

The coloured blocks rearrange to reveal the ENDER DRAGON!

Crossword answers:
- ¹ BLAZE
- ² GHAST
- ³ WITHER
- WARDEN
- ⁴ VILLAGER
- ⁵ PHANTOM
- ⁶ SPIDER
- ⁷ PIGLIN
- ⁸ SKELETON
- ⁹ ENDERMAN
- ¹⁰ CREEPER
- ¹¹ ZOMBIE
- ¹² DROWNED
- ¹³ WITCH

Page 17 - The Word Mine

The missing block is... OBSIDIAN

Page 48-49 - Craft-y Quiz

1: B	5: A	9: C	13: A	17: C
2: A	6: C	10: B	14: A	18: A
3: C	7: C	11: B	15: A	19: B
4: C	8: B	12: C	16: B	20: B

How did you get on?

0-5
It looks like you're new to this, but if you've read this far then you should have picked up a few things to help get you started.

5-10
You're getting good at this. Keep trying new things and you'll be an expert in no time!

11-15
Impressive work. Award yourself 'diamond' status and craft yourself a new armour suit.

15-19
Wow! You seriously know your stuff. You probably dream in little square blocks.

20
You're either good with Google or a **Minecraft master!**

Congratulations!